D1062623

Secret America

Secret American History

From Witch Trials to Internment Camps

by Norman Pearl

Consultant:
Jessica Martin, PhD
History Department
University of Colorado, Boulder

Capstone
press

Mankato, Minnesota

Edge Books are published by Capstone Press,
151 Good Counsel Drive, P.O. Box 669, Mankato, Minnesota 56002.
www.capstonepress.com

Books published by Capstone Press are manufactured with paper
containing at least 10 percent post-consumer waste.

Library of Congress Cataloging-in-Publication Data
Pearl, Norman.
   Secret American history: from witch trials to internment camps /
by Norman Pearl.
   p. cm. — (Edge books. Secret America)
   Summary: "Describes a variety of secret and mysterious events in
the United States" — Provided by publisher.
   Includes bibliographical references and index.
   ISBN 978-1-4296-3360-4 (library binding)
   1. United States — History — Miscellanea — Juvenile literature.
2. Curiosities and wonders — United States — Juvenile literature.
3. Secrecy — United States — Miscellanea — Juvenile literature.
I. Title.
E178.3.P425 2010
973 — dc22   2009005732

Editorial Credits

Kathryn Clay, editor; Tracy Davies, designer; Eric Gohl, media researcher

Photo Credits

AP Images, 25; AP Images/National Park Service, cover (left), 18; Corbis/Bettmann, 16;
Courtesy of the Runestone Museum, 6, 7; Courtesy of the Salem Witch Museum, Salem,
Massachusetts, 11; Courtesy Ronald Reagan Library, 19; DVIC, cover (background), 20,
28; Getty Images Inc./Time Life Pictures/Hank Walker, 24; Getty Images Inc./Time Life
Pictures/National Archives, cover (middle), 23; Getty Images Inc./Time Life Pictures/
Thomas D. Mcavoy, 26; Library of Congress, 15, 17, 21, 22; NASA, 4, 27; North Wind
Picture Archives, cover (right), 8, 10, 12, 13, 14; Shutterstock/Cobalt Moon Design,
(patriotic background design element); Shutterstock/digitalife, (banners design
element); Shutterstock/Janaka, (paper design element); Shutterstock/PKruger,
(cobbled road design element); Shutterstock/Sergey Kandakov, (black paper design
element); Shutterstock/Sibrikov Valery, (old paper design element); Shutterstock/
velora, (wax seal design element)

Table of Contents

The Mystery of History

If you think history is boring, you may not have all the facts yet. Sometimes we aren't told the whole truth. Other times, stories are created to make a point. Maybe you heard that George Washington chopped down a cherry tree and refused to lie about it? Well, that never happened.

America's history is filled with mystery. This book is all about revealing the facts of the past. But many questions about American history remain unanswered. In these cases, it's up to you to review the facts. Then you can decide what to believe.

A Mysterious Stone

Edge Fact:

Rocks found in Minnesota look like the anchors Vikings used to secure their boats.

Olaf Ohman discovered the Kensington Runestone on his farm.

Who was the first European explorer to reach North America? For a long time, people believed it was Christopher Columbus.

Researchers recently learned that Viking explorers from Scandinavia arrived more than 100 years before Columbus. People first thought the Vikings stayed near the Atlantic Ocean's coast. But mysterious items found in the Midwest might prove that the Vikings traveled much farther inland.

The Kensington Runestone is a stone that stands 31 inches (79 centimeters) high. It weighs 202 pounds (92 kilograms). In 1898, a farmer and his son found the stone just north of Kensington, Minnesota. The stone is covered with ancient Viking symbols called runes. The runes tell the story of Vikings who traveled west.

But not everyone agrees that the stone is real. Most language experts think the stone is a fake. In 2004, the runestone was displayed at a museum in Sweden. Experts there disagreed on whether or not the stone was real. **Geologists** have also studied the stone. They think the stone could date back to the early 1300s. For now, the creator of the Kensington Runestone remains a mystery.

geologist — someone who studies minerals, rocks, and soil

That's One Tall Viking!

The Kensington Runestone can be seen at the Runestone Museum in Alexandria, Minnesota. In a nearby park, visitors can have their picture taken with Big Ole. Big Ole is a 28-foot (8.5-meter) Viking statue weighing more than 4 tons (3.6 metric tons).

The Lost Colony of Roanoke

Captain John White found the word "croatoan" carved into a tree.

In 1587, a group of people from England boarded a ship. The men, women, and children planned to start a town on Roanoke Island in North Carolina. But soon after landing, the **colonists** ran out of supplies.

Captain John White returned to England for more supplies. But England was at war with Spain, and ships were only being used for battles. White was unable to return to Roanoke for two years.

When he did return, White was shocked by what he found. The growing colony had disappeared. A single clue was left behind. The word "croatoan" was carved on a tree.

What happened to the colonists? One idea is that they left to settle elsewhere. Others believe Croatoan Indians killed the colonists. But it's more likely that the Indians offered to help the colonists. The Indians had enough food to keep the colonists alive. Years later, Indians with gray eyes were seen in the area. Some spoke English and had English names. It's possible they were related to the Roanoke colonists.

colonist — someone who lives in a newly settled area

Still Searching

Although most experts think the colonists went with the Indians, they want to be sure. Researchers plan to use DNA testing to crack this case. They put together a list of people who might be related to the lost colonists. The researchers hope to test DNA samples from these people to prove their ideas.

3

The Salem Witch Trials

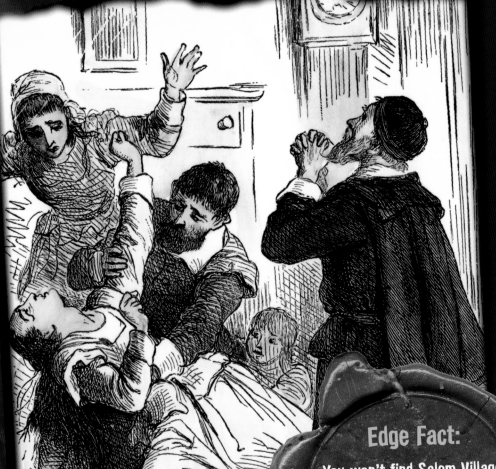

Reverend Cotton Mather (right) prayed for the girls he thought were bewitched.

Edge Fact:

You won't find Salem Village on any maps. Shortly after the trials, the town changed its name to Danvers.

In January 1692, two girls in Salem Village, Massachusetts, suddenly began acting strangely. Betty Parris and Abigail Williams screamed and threw fits. By February, two more girls were acting strangely. Ann Putnam and Elizabeth Hubbard claimed invisible spirits were pinching them.

No one knew what was causing this strange behavior. Some people thought Tituba Indian, a slave woman, had taught the girls about magic. Because most villagers were **Puritans**, magic was strictly forbidden. The girls may have become frightened after trying to cast spells. Doctors feared the girls had been bewitched.

The girls accused villagers of being witches. More than 100 people were arrested. Nineteen people were found guilty of witchcraft and put to death.

Puritan — a follower of a strict religion common during the 1500s and 1600s

Tituba's Confession

Tituba was one of the first people to be accused. She quickly admitted to being a witch. Tituba knew she would not be put to death if she confessed. Her confession may have encouraged the entire witch hunt.

Some historians think the girls had **ergot** poisoning. That would explain their strange behavior. Others blame greed. People found guilty of witchcraft lost their property. Some of the accused owned large plots of land. People wanting to buy this land didn't care if the owners were guilty or not. Meanwhile, the girls enjoyed being the center of attention.

One thing is certain. Nineteen people died because the girls created a panic. Suspected witches were later freed. But this didn't help the people who had already been put to death.

ergot — a fungus that grows on grain

The Proctor Story

Salem Village citizen John Proctor did not believe the girls and spoke out. When Proctor called them liars, the girls accused his wife of witchcraft. Proctor tried to defend his wife, but then the girls accused him of witchcraft. John and his wife were jailed, and he was sentenced to death. His sentence was carried out on August 19, 1692.

Edge Fact:

The youngest person accused of witchcraft was only 4 years old.

4

Road to Freedom

Runaway slaves were often chased
by slave catchers and dogs.

Edge Fact:
Former slave Harriet
Tubman helped rescue
about 300 slaves.

14

Three slaves attempted to escape in the pitch-black night. Lanterns glowed behind them. Dogs barked in the distance. Slave catchers were near. But the slaves kept running. They were determined to reach the Underground Railroad. If they made it, the slaves might secure their freedom.

The Underground Railroad was a series of homes and shelters in the southern United States. It operated from about 1810 to 1840. People who disagreed with slavery created the route. They hid runaway slaves in their cellars, attics, and barns. They also gave runaways food and clothing.

With the help of the Underground Railroad, more than 100,000 people escaped slavery. They fled to the northern United States and to Canada, where slavery was illegal.

The Underground Railroad had to operate in complete secrecy. Anyone caught hiding slaves had to pay a fine. Runaways who were caught were often beaten, tortured, or even killed. But slaves were willing to risk death for the chance at freedom.

Mr. President

Levi Coffin was known as the president of the Underground Railroad. His home was called Grand Central Station. Runaways were welcome there day or night. Coffin and his wife hid more than 2,000 slaves.

Levi Coffin

What Killed President Garfield?

President James Garfield (center) was shot at a train station on July 2, 1881.

It was a hot July day in 1881. U.S. President James Garfield had been in office four months. As Garfield waited to catch a train, Charles Guiteau shot the president in the back.

Dr. Willard Bliss was the first doctor on the scene. He pushed a metal instrument into Garfield's wound to find the bullet. This only made the wound bigger. Then Bliss stuck his unwashed finger into the wound. At that time, doctors didn't know this could lead to an infection.

Other doctors tried to treat the president. A total of 16 doctors poked at the wound. When they were done, the bullet wound had grown into a large infected area.

On September 19, 1881, Garfield died. He had been in terrible pain for months. An **autopsy** showed that the bullet wound was not life threatening. It was the infection that killed him. Had his doctors left him alone, Garfield probably would have lived.

autopsy — an examination performed after someone dies to find the cause of death

Blaming the Doctors

The man who shot Garfield also blamed the doctors. At his trial, Charles Guiteau claimed to be innocent. He said the president's death was the doctors' fault. Many people agreed with Guiteau, but he was still found guilty.

Charles Guiteau

Japanese Internment Camps

Barbed wire fences surrounded the Japanese internment camps.

On December 7, 1941, the Japanese military bombed Pearl Harbor. The United States responded by declaring war on Japan. Two months later, President Franklin Roosevelt issued Executive Order 9066. This order meant that about 120,000 Japanese Americans would be forced from their homes. They were shipped to one of 10 internment camps across the western United States.

A Late Apology

Almost 50 years later, the U.S. government admitted that the internment camps were unjust. Former prisoners received $20,000 and a signed apology from President Ronald Reagan.

People worried that the Japanese Americans were enemy spies. It didn't matter that many were United States citizens or that half of them were children. Most had never even been to Japan.

At the camps, Japanese Americans were treated like prisoners. Armed guards stood watch day and night.

Edge Fact:

Children in the camps formed baseball teams and Boy Scout troops.

Life in the camps was difficult. The food and housing were poor. Many of the cold, dirty shelters once held cattle or horses. People died because of low-quality medical care.

Some Japanese Americans were held in the camps more than four years. After being released, they were given free transportation and $25. They tried to return to their homes, but most of their property had been sold.

The Manhattan Project

The atomic bomb dropped on August 9, 1945, created a large mushroom-shaped cloud.

The Manhattan Project was a top secret military project. Its purpose was to produce the world's first atomic bomb. By 1942, the need for the bomb seemed clear. U.S. soldiers were fighting in World War II (1939–1945). It was rumored that Germany was building an atomic bomb. The United States was determined to build the bomb first.

The nation's best scientists and engineers were hired to develop the powerful bomb. Well-known companies like Pan American Airways and General Electric were also involved. In all, more than 125,000 workers built parts for the bomb. But only a few people understood what they were doing. Scientists and engineers often spoke in code. The bomb itself was referred to as the "gadget."

Edge Fact:

The total cost of the Manhattan Project was about $2 billion.

Sharing Secrets

The United States government didn't want other countries to know how to build atomic bombs. They tried to keep the information secret. But in 1950, scientist Klaus Fuchs was arrested for sharing secrets with the Soviet Union. In 1951, Julius and Ethel Rosenberg were also arrested for sharing bomb-making secrets with spies. People still debate whether or not this couple was guilty.

Ethel and Julius Rosenberg

Three research centers were created. One center was located in Los Alamos, New Mexico. Under the direction of J. Robert Oppenheimer, four atomic bombs were produced there. Two of these bombs were dropped over Japan in August 1945. More than 100,000 innocent people were killed by the bombs. Many others suffered serious health problems.

The powerful bombs worked as planned. Six days after the second bomb was dropped, the Japanese surrendered.

A Big Decision

President Harry Truman gave the order to drop the bombs. He said it was the only way to make Japan surrender. Other people argued that it was unacceptable to cause the deaths of so many innocent people.

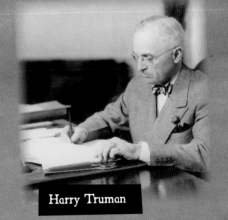

Harry Truman

Edge Fact:

Each atomic bomb had the explosive power of about 20,000 tons (18,000 metric tons) of dynamite.

A Communist Scare

Senator Joe McCarthy accused hundreds of government workers of being communists.

During the 1940s, panic swept through the United States. Citizens feared the spread of **communism**. The Soviet Union was a communist nation. Its government controlled TV stations and newspapers. People were punished for their religious beliefs. Americans did not want this to happen in the United States.

A group of goverment workers tried to find communists in the United States. The workers accused people of being traitors and spies. Being a communist wasn't against the law. But it did mean you could lose your job and your friends. Frightened people accused others to help themselves. Some people were jailed for refusing to name suspected communists.

Senator Joe McCarthy claimed he had a list of 200 communists who worked for the government. But no one ever saw the list. The act of accusing people without proof is now known as McCarthyism. The government later said that McCarthy's behavior was wrong. But this was after many lives were ruined.

Edge Fact:

Many historians compare the communist scare to the Salem witch trials.

communism — a political system based on government ownership of all land and industry

Hollywood Targets

Hollywood entertainers were major targets during the communist scare. More than 300 actors, directors, and writers were on a secret list. People on the list were suspected communists. They had trouble getting jobs, and their careers were destroyed.

accused Hollywood entertainers

War Criminals Welcomed

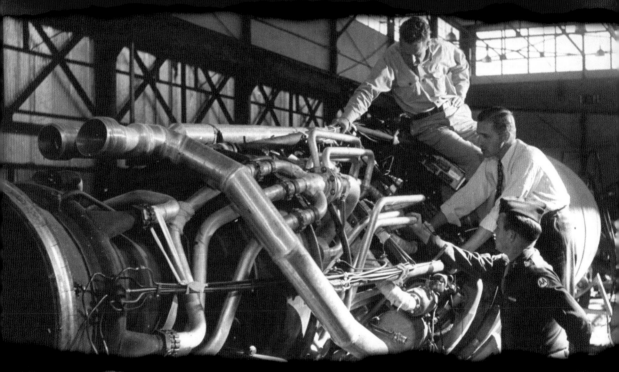

German scientists who came to the United States after World War II helped develop military weapons.

During World War II (1939–1945), German scientists invented several new technologies including the V-2 rocket and other military weapons. Some of these scientists were also members of Germany's **Nazi Party.**

New Technologies

With the help of German scientists, the United States became the first country to land on the moon. German scientists also helped develop medicine, missiles, and chemical weapons.

After the war, many Nazis were sent to jail. But some people in the U.S. government did not want the scientists jailed. They hoped the scientists would work for them instead. But people with questionable pasts were not allowed in the United States. This created a difficult problem.

To get the scientists into the country, U.S. military officials created false records. In all, more than 450 German scientists **immigrated** to the United States. U.S. government officials were willing to look the other way as long as the scientists agreed to help them.

Edge Fact:
Skilled Nazi spies were also secretly brought into the United States.

Nazi Party — the German political party led by Adolf Hitler

immigrate — to come from one country to live in another country

27

Finding the Truth

America's history is filled with interesting events. Some of them are well documented in history books. Others are surrounded by secrecy. This book has listed some of America's secret history, but there is much more to discover.

Now it's your turn to dig up some secret history. Talk to your teachers, parents, or librarians. Ask if there are any interesting secrets about your town. Or check out old copies of your hometown newspaper. You'll be amazed by all the secrets you can uncover.

Glossary

atomic bomb (uh-TOM-ik BOM) — a powerful bomb that explodes with great force; atomic bombs destroy large areas and leave behind dangerous radiation.

autopsy (AW-top-see) — an examination performed on a dead body to find the cause of death

colonist (KAH-luh-nist) — someone who lives in a newly settled area

communism (KAHM-yuh-nis-um) — a political system based on government ownership of all land and industry

DNA (dee-en-AY) — material in cells that gives people their individual characteristics; DNA stands for deoxyribonucleic acid.

ergot (UR-gut) — a fungus that grows on grains

geologist (jee-AHL-uh-jist) — someone who studies minerals, rocks, and soil

immigrate (IM-uh-grate) — to come from one country to live permanently in another country

Nazi Party (NOT-see PAR-tee) — the German political party led by Adolph Hitler; the Nazis ruled Germany from 1933 to 1945.

Puritan (PYOOR-uh-tuhn) — a follower of a strict religion common during the 1500s and 1600s; Puritans wanted simple church services and enforced a strict moral code.

traitor (TRAY-tur) — someone who aids the enemy of his or her country

Read More

Burgan, Michael. *The Underground Railroad*. Slavery in the Americas. New York: Chelsea House, 2006.

Landau, Elaine. *Witness the Salem Witchcraft Trials with Elaine Landau*. Explore Colonial America with Elaine Landau. Berkeley Heights, N.J.: Enslow, 2006.

Miller, Lee. *Roanoke: The Mystery of the Lost Colony*. New York: Scholastic Nonfiction, 2007.

Internet Sites

FactHound offers a safe, fun way to find Internet sites related to this book. All of the sites on FactHound have been researched by our staff.

Here's all you do:

Visit *www.facthound.com*

FactHound will fetch the best sites for you!

Index

24080 0433